GW01044091

Naughty Games For Grown-ups

Jenny Thomson

NAUGHTY GAMES FOR GROWN-UPS
1st edition printed in 2002

Text by Jenny Thomson

Illustrations by Rob Smith

Summersdale Publishers Ltd
46 West Street
Chichester
West Sussex
PO19 1RP
UK

www.summersdale.com

Printed and bound by TWP

ISBN: 1-84024-432-1
ISBN 13: 978-1-84024-432-8

Contents

Introduction

Naughty Games for Grown-ups is on a mission. A mission of sexual exploration. A quest to banish boring sex lives forever.

Yes, it's time to put on your sexiest underwear, get out that whip and indulge in some dirty talk.

If you like a bit of sauce, enjoy being raunchy and don't mind getting down and dirty, then you've come to the right place. There are a range of sex games waiting for you in this book, from the tame to the downright X-rated. There are games for couples, and for mixed/all male/all female groups.

All the games have been tried and tested by a willing author.

Chapter One
Foreplay

When you hear the word 'foreplay', do you immediately think of your partner nibbling on your ear like it's a Mars Bar and whispering sweet nothings? Stop worrying that they'll bite through your earlobe and wipe off that spittle because you're in for a surprise. A saucy surprise.

It's time to try out some new methods of foreplay. Things that will really get you in the mood before you take your clothes off.

Rating – Just a light warm-up
with risqué overtones.

Scavenger Hunt

How to play:

Hide a small item on your person. The other player has to hunt for it. If that means that they have to look in your pants, then how can you say no? It's all part of the game. Ooh, I say.

The Rules:

Rules, shmules. There are no rules.

Make the game more interesting by:

Playing it when you're in a public place (e.g. at the cinema).

Tip:

Don't play this game when you're having dinner at your mum's. You'll knock over the gravy jug with all that jigging.

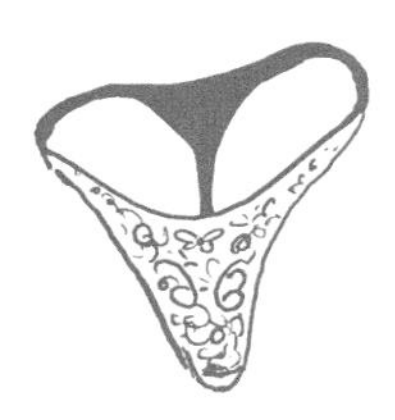

Truth or Bare

How to play:

You or your partner says something like, 'I once had sex in the stationery cupboard at work', or 'I call my left breast/penis Charlie', and the other has to guess whether or not it's true. If you guess right, they have to remove an item of clothing – if you're wrong, you have to bare.

This is a game to really get you going.

Examples:

'I lost my virginity when I was fourteen.'
'I once dressed up as a dominatrix.'

'I once got arrested for having sex in the park.'
'I'd like to go outside wearing absolutely nothing under a big coat.'
'I like going out wearing a dress and no knickers.'*

*Hopefully it won't be your boyfriend who says this.

Tip:

This isn't a good time to say something like, 'True or false? I'm giving your best mate one.'

Sex on the Box

How to play:

Get cosy whilst watching your favourite TV programme. Every time a character does a particular action, you have to do a pre-agreed action yourself. For example, every time *The A-Team*'s Hannibal lights up a cigar, a breast gets squeezed. Joey says 'How you doin'?' and it's hand-down-the-pants time. Pat Butcher appears with a new pair of earrings and you have to give your partner a lovebite.

Tip:

If one of the *Sex and the City* gals gets laid, you do too.

Make the game more interesting by:

Watching a late night film on Channel 5 or renting a naughty video. Pick a character and copy their every move with your partner.

The rules:

If you miss your cue, you have to do what you were meant to do either during the adverts or after the show.

Naked Tongue-go

How to play:

This is French kissing with a difference. Set that stopwatch to go and stick your tongue down your partner's throat. Whoever lasts longest gets to be licked in their favourite place.

The rules:

No tickling your partner or touching them in a particular place so that they'll pull out of the kiss. That's cheating.

Make the game more interesting by:

Offering a very special reward to the person who wins the most games (you have to dress up as their fantasy figure).

Getting the loser to pay a forfeit (they have to kiss you all over your naked body).

Tip:

Make sure that your partner is not having difficulty breathing. This game is about seduction, not resuscitation.

Chapter Two
Double the Fun

If you're a woman looking for new ways of spicing up your love life then you've come to the right place. If you're a bloke aiming to hit the right note then this chapter is for you.

It's time to get down to some risqué business.

To take part in these games for couples you must have lots of naughty thoughts, absolutely no shame, and the ability to remove your partner's pants with your teeth.

Rating – Fantasy sex, only real.

The Fantasy Draw

How to play:

Make up a list of your ultimate sexual fantasies. You pick one of his and he picks one of yours – it's show time.

Some sexual fantasies to try:

Making love to your favourite film star.
Dressing up as a cowgirl and being Annie Oakley to his Jesse James.
Getting hot with a fireman and his hose.
Dressing up as a schoolteacher and a naughty pupil.

Pretending that you come from an Amazonian tribe and have kidnapped your partner. He or she is now your sex slave.
Pretending that you're still a virgin and your partner is teaching you the art of making love.
Dressing as a dominatrix. If your man doesn't want to please you, get out that whip.
Stopping traffic as a corrupt cop who's just handcuffed a suspect and is offering freedom in exchange for sexual favours.*

*Impersonating a police officer is a criminal offence so leave it to the privacy of your own bedroom.

Getting to Know You

How to play:

How much do you really know about your partner's sexual peccadilloes? Or more importantly, how much do they know about yours?

Take turns at sexing each other out by asking questions about your erotic lives and experiences.

This is the perfect game to play with someone who's had a few sexual partners.

Possible questions:

Have you ever had sex in a public place, and if so where?

Which famous person would you most like to sleep with?

How old were you when you lost your virginity?

Have you ever shaved off your pubic hair?

Have you ever had a threesome?

What's the longest you've gone without it?

Have you ever fantasised about being the opposite sex?

What's your favourite part of sex?

Just for him:

What's the most embarrassing erection you've ever had?
Are you a boobs or bum man?
Have you ever squeezed a male mate's bum?
Have you ever accidentally exposed yourself?

Just for her:

Have you ever flirted with another woman?
Have you ever flirted with a man to get something out of him, like a job or money?
Have your boobs ever accidentally escaped from your top and given people an eyeful?

All Steamed Up

How to play:

Play this in the shower or bath.

You have to wash each other without using your hands. This is the only time in your relationship that you'll get to wash his face with your breasts.

The point? There is none. But hey, by the end of this you won't care.

Get him all steamed up by:

Drying him afterwards using a tiny towel. Well, that way it'll take you longer to give him a rub down.

Tip:

It's unwise to do this if you live in a bedsit where there are ten people queuing to get into the bathroom at any given time.

Randy Raffle

How to play:

Write your own love tokens, put them in a hat and pick one each. You win what's on the token.

The rules:

Love tokens can be as racy or as romantic as you like.

Love tokens:

A candle-lit dinner for two.
A night devoted to just you.

A foot massage.
A sexual fantasy fulfilled.
To be covered in chocolate body paint and have it all licked off (by your partner, of course, unless you want to involve the neighbours).
To watch a blue movie and re-enact some of the scenes of your choice.
To have a sex toy of your choice used on you.

Breathless

How to play:

Partners have to remove the other person's pants with their teeth. The prize is underneath.

The rules:

No biting the flesh (unless your partner likes it). Thongs can be worn, but they must be visible without the use of a microscope.

Make it more fun by:

Allowing each player just thirty seconds to get the other's underwear off.

Wearing edible panties.
Wearing vibrating pants for that great sensation on the lips and the mouth.

Tips:

Pants must be clean. No one wants to go to casualty with knicker-poisoning.

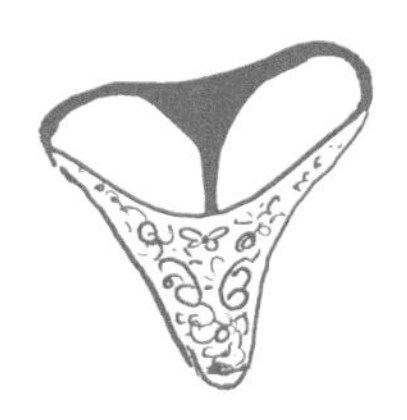

Chapter Three
A Touch of Sauce

If your relationship is more floppy than flambé, and a hot night consists of turning up the electric blanket, it's about time this book came to the rescue with a touch of sauce. Let the games begin.

Rating – Let's just say that you'll have a smile on your face and a spring in your step if you carry on like this.

Tombola

Preparation:

Get some raffle tickets. Get some saucy prizes. Put aforementioned saucy prizes on display with numbers on them (putting them on show will really get you in the mood to put on a bit of a show yourself) and then let the game commence.

How to play:

Put the raffle tickets in your bra (if you're not too ticklish). Take it in turns to take a ticket. Will your lucky number come up?

Possible prizes:

A little glow in the dark rubber number
Furry handcuffs
Edible body lotion
A pair of rubber pants with a 'hung like a donkey' pouch
An all over (and I do mean *all* over) massage
A gift voucher for Ann Summers
Suspenders

Tip:

Make sure that when you're playing you don't accidentally leave one of your prizes beside your donation for the church tombola. The vicar will not be expecting to get a vibrating bra.

Ice Cream

Preparation:

Buy as many different flavours of ice cream as you can.

How to play:

Your partner smears ice cream on a part of their body. You have to lick it off slowly whilst blindfolded and try to guess the flavour. Guess right and it's your turn to be licked.

The rules:

What rules? You can lick as much ice cream off your partner as you want. Mmmmmm.

Get saucy by:

Getting out the strawberries. Well, you need something to eat with all that yummy ice cream.
Blindfolding your partner with a silk scarf.

Tip:

Be prepared to get messy. You'll both get so hot the ice cream will melt.

Chapter Four
Some Old Favourites

If you want to pin the tail on something far more interesting than a donkey, or would take great delight in achieving 'orgasm' on a triple word score in *Scrabble*, this is the chapter for you.

Traditional games have gone saucy. Use the games you loved or hated as a kid to spice up your sex life. Guaranteed.

Rating – These games may be based on wholesome family favourites but they're definitely not for when your parents come round.

Pin the Tail on the Donkey

Preparation:

No donkey needed, just a drawing of a naked man (make him as big as a donkey if you like) or a blown-up picture from *Hot Hunks in Manly Trunks*. You also need a picture of a woman for him.

How to play:

Get a pin and whatever body part of the man you hit when you're blindfolded you have to suck, fondle or lick on your partner. He has to do the same with you when he pins his lady.

Make him purr by:

Putting the names of sexual treats next to body parts.

Saucy Snakes and Ladders

You will need:

Two long dextrous tongues (you'll find out why later)
Somewhere to go down on your hands and knees

How to play:

When you have to go down a snake it's a case of getting down on your knees and pleasuring your partner.

Go up a ladder and it's the top half of their body you have to lavish (or should that be ravish?) with attention.

Make the snake rise by:

Awarding special prizes to certain snakes and ladders.

You'll love this game because:

If you don't have the *Snakes and Ladders* board game you can go out and buy one and the seller won't know that you're going to use it as a sex toy. Kinky or what?

Tip:

This is not the night to wear your big, thick, bullet-proof knickers. You know the ones – even *you* have trouble pulling them down.

Naked Monopoly

How to play:

Old rules apply until it comes to landing on your partner's property. When you do they get a piece of your property: an item of clothing. The same happens when he lands on yours.

See if you can last until you get naked before you ditch Mayfair for more fun pursuits.

Sex it up by:

Making different squares you land on have prizes or forfeits attached. If you land on the Go to Jail square, you get a conjugal visit. Bond Street and he has to dress up as James Bond and seduce you. Land on Free Parking and you get to snog like teenagers. The possibilities are endless...

Tip:

Cheat when your partner's not looking. That way, they'll be naked first... and your plaything.

Naked Bingo

How to play:

Choose a naughty prize for whoever shouts 'house' first.

Make bingo sexy by:

Allocating some little surprises if certain numbers are called.

Prizes:

One fat lady – he gets to squeeze one of your breasts or you get to squeeze his bum

Legs eleven – a thigh gets stroked
Two little ducks, twenty-two – whoever gets it has to moon
Heinz fifty-seven – you have to do 57 different manoeuvres in the bedroom
Clickety-click, sixty-six – take off your bra
Sixty-nine – if you don't know what to do for this one then please read *Sexual Positions for Beginners*
Two fat ladies, eighty-eight – you have to put your breasts in his face

Tip:

Don't tell your gran that you're going to be playing bingo. She'll only turn up in her best coat and expect you to give her a lift to the nearest Mecca.

Blind Man in the Buff

How to play:

This is a great game to play in a group (if you're looking for ideas for your next orgy that is).

Play this like the old game, only everyone has to be naked (or in their skimpies if they're shy).

The rules:

The same rules apply except that when someone gets caught a grope is most definitely not out of the question. Identities are guessed by bums and chests being groped.

Tip:

This could be a good way of breaking the ice with the neighbours. If you invite them round to play they'll think you're nuts and call the police. But you can be assured that they will have got to know you better.

Naked Twister

Preparation:

Get out that old *Twister* mat and get the game rolling. Or if you're playing it with friends, get them to bring their *Twister* mats and join them all together.

How to play:

Every time you fall down you have to remove a piece of clothing.

Take the game to a new level:

Award prizes to your partner each time they land on a certain colour.

If you're playing it as a group, whenever a girl lands on a certain colour, all the girls have to do a forfeit together, and vice-versa for the guys.

Forfeits:

Moon
Perform a role-play with someone of the opposite sex
Pole dance
Fake an orgasm
Kiss the feet of everyone of the opposite sex

Saucy Scrabble

How to play:

Play as usual but every word must be saucy, sexy or just downright filthy.

The rules:

Words are only allowed if you've both heard of them. Slang is in as long as the word is rude.

Make this game hot by:

If anyone has any tiles left over they have to touch a part of their partner's body beginning with that letter. This applies to every letter they have left over.

For her:

Playing the game dressed as a schoolgirl (don't forget the pigtails) will reduce your partner to a quivering wreck and make it easier for you to win. Sneaky.

Chapter Five
Card Games

When you think of card games, you probably think of old men playing poker in smoky bars, or playing *Snap* with your brat of a brother in games that always ended in tears. But card games can be sexy. Very sexy.

By the time you've tried out my naughty card games you'll see why.

Rating – Card games for grown-ups.

'If'

How to play:

For this game you will need a pack of cards and no inhibitions.

Shuffle the cards and then halve them between you. Then take turns at turning over cards. But there's a forfeit that comes with each...

Ace – your partner holds all the aces here. They get to choose what you do
King – nuzzle the neck
Queen – a French kiss
Jack – stroke your partner's thigh

Terrific Ten – stroke the body part of your partner's choice
Naughty Nine – it's nipple-playing time
Eyeful Eight – you have to remove an item of clothing
Sinful Seven – kiss your partner in an intimate place
Sexy Six – you have to re-enact a scene from a film of your partner's choice
Fantasy Five – you have to play out one of your partner's fantasies
Fruity Four – devour a piece of fruit or chocolate in the sexiest way possible
Thrilling Three – give them a thrill: use your mouth to bring your partner to fever pitch
Teasing Two – do a sexy striptease

Strip Poker

How to play:

The dealer gives each player five cards and puts the rest of the pack face down on the table. Each player looks at their cards and keeps the cards that are of the same suit (preferably) or number. They exchange the cards they don't want by placing them face down in a new pile, and taking new cards from the original one.

What you're really looking for is two, three or four of a kind. In the event of a tie, the highest card wins (ace being the highest all the way down to two being the lowest). The object of the game is to get as many matching cards as you can. You've got a full house when you have three of one kind and two of the other.

Lose a hand: lose an item of clothing. First one naked loses.

Tip:

Wear a sexy surprise under your clothes. Say a garter, g-string or suspenders. And for her...

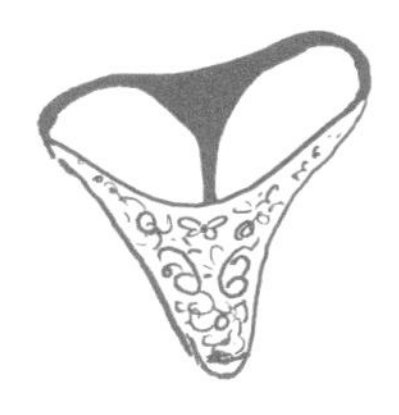

Pair Off

How to play:

Divide the cards equally amongst the players.

Taking turns, each player has to show one of their cards to the other players. If another player has the same number they are now a couple and have to do something together.

The couple that pair off have to:

Give everybody else a talk on what happens between a man and a woman, with a demonstration.

Flirt with each other like they've only just met.

Give the rest of the room a lesson on the different types of kissing.
Act like they've got a strange fetish (like they want to bonk everybody's shoes).

Tip:

Pray that you don't end up having to snog the guy with the fish mouth.

Chapter Six
Girls Only

For this girls' night you need to get equipped. Put on your best gear. Get all glam. And if you get a few drinks inside you before you start, even better.

You'll need to get some props for these games. Fix yourself up with: a naked man; a pair of handcuffs for you and your mates; a willy that's not attached to a man; a blow-up man for everyone.

Ready? Grab your coat; it's time to go.

Rating – Games to make that hen night or girls' night go with a swing.

Strip Hangman

Preparation:

For this game you need a guy. He can be a real one (borrowed, paid for or stolen). Or if you don't want a slap from your best mate/to be dumped by your man for bonking the stripper/to get arrested, you can always use a dummy or a blow-up doll.

You can't play strip hangman unless you've got some clothes to take off him. So if it's not a walking and talking man you're using, make sure you sort out the clothes beforehand.

The rules:

Usual hangman rules apply except for one thing. Every phrase picked has to have something to do with sex or your naughty bits. That means things like the film *9½ Weeks*, and sex toys like the Rampant Rabbit Vibrator as featured on *Sex and the City*.

Reach fever pitch by:

Hiring a stripper dressed as a fireman to play with (make sure he's got a big hose). Will you be the one to take off his pants with your teeth?

How to play:

Every time someone guesses the right word she gets to remove an item of his clothing.* Lucky girl.

*This will get in some practice for later.

Tip:

If you're hiring a stripper, make sure that he comes with a money back guarantee in case he, erm, doesn't perform to his full capacity. You didn't organise this get together to look at something that's so small it should be on the end of a cocktail stick.

Drink or Divulge

Preparation:

Line up the cocktails. Make the kinky-sounding ones: Orgasm, Slippery Nipple, Sex on the Beach, Girl on Top, Going Down, Virgin's Choice and Sex Bomb.

How to play:

Each player has a choice. Drink what's in the glass in one go or answer a very personal question.

Go for the question and it's time to choose a category. The choices are: sex, relationships or confessions.

The rules:

Even if you tell the truth, if the rest of the girls think you're lying you have to take a drink.

Sex questions:

What did you really think the first time you had sex?
What's the best/worst thing your boyfriend does in bed?
Have you ever faked an orgasm? Do it now.
What's the kinkiest thing you've ever done in bed?
What's the kinkiest thing you'd like to do in bed?
What's your most embarrassing sex moment?
When was the last time you had sex when you shouldn't have? Give details.

What's your oral sex technique?
If you had to sleep with one of your teachers from school, who would it be and why?
Would you sleep with someone for money? How much would you want?

Relationship questions:

What's the worst thing you've ever done to a friend/a man/a relative?
What's the most annoying habit your best friend/boyfriend has? Do it now if you can.
If your mates didn't like your boyfriend would you dump him?
Have you ever refused to go out with someone because their dress sense was so bad?

Confessions:

What's the most embarrassing thing you've ever done?
Have you ever stolen anything?
Have you ever conned your way into a job?
What's the biggest lie you've ever told a friend/boyfriend/your mum?
Have you ever fancied or slept with your boyfriend's best mate?

I Went to the Sex Shop and I Bought...

Preparation:

Cruise a sex shop (either online or on your feet) to give you an idea of the things you can buy there.

How to play:

One girl starts with: 'I went to the sex shop and I bought a twelve-inch vibrator.' The girl next to her has to repeat the same sentence but add a purchase of her own. The person after her does the same and so on as the list gets longer and more difficult to remember.

The rules:

Purchases mentioned don't have to be real things. The more unlikely and downright dirty the better.

If someone forgets a product they have to pay a penalty.

Penalties:

Wear a willy-shaped hat for the rest of the evening.

Sing a sexy song. Try Madonna's 'Like a Virgin'.

Pretend to be a man and chat up one of your friends. (If you're out on the town you have to chat up a complete stranger.)

Stuff a cucumber down your pants so it'll look like you've got a willy.

Impersonate your boyfriend having an orgasm. Tell everyone in the room how to perform oral sex as though they've no idea what it is, never mind how to do it.

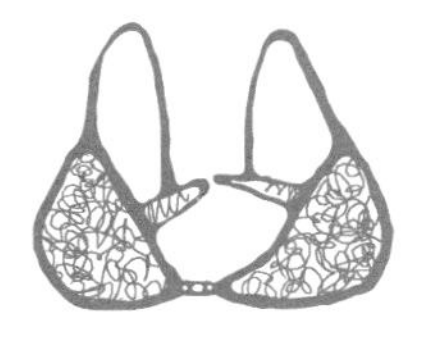

Ring the Thing

Preparation:

You'll need something shaped like a man's favourite body part for this game (and we're not talking about their brains).

If you're really stuck you can always make one out of papier mâché, plaster or join a pottery class especially (you can just imagine the horrified look on everybody's faces when they realise that you are not making a lopsided teapot). Whatever you make, it must be big enough to throw rings around it.

How to play:

Each girl takes it in turns to have three tries at throwing a ring over the penis. Whoever succeeds gets a naughty prize: an erotic book, a collection of sex tips, or rude-shaped chocolate.

Tip:

You can't use a real man for this. No man can stay erect and stand still for that long. (If you find one who can, hold onto him.)

Talking Dirty

Preparation:

This is a word association game, so all you need to play is a very dirty mind and an extensive sexual vocabulary.

How to play:

Sit in a circle. Starting with A, each girl has to think of a word to do with sex beginning with the next letter in the alphabet. (A: Arousal, B: Breasts, C: Crotchless knickers...)

If anyone falters they have to do a forfeit.

Forfeits:

Describe your first sexual experience
Get frisky with a carrot
Put a condom on a banana
Fake an orgasm
Do a sexy dance and be awarded marks for performance
Rank past lovers by sexual performance
Describe your best sexual manoeuvre

Chapter Seven
Guys Only

Looking for a booze-filled night with your mates? Haven't been near a woman in a long time? Have a thing about women's knickers (including the fact that you just want to get into them whenever possible)?

Then these games are for you.

Cheers!

Rating – A booze-up with balls.

Truth or Drink

Before you get busy:

Make a noxious concoction of beer and spirits and stir well.

How to play:

Everyone has to answer a sex question. Whoever bottles out has to drink from the glass.

Possible questions:

How old were you when you first got laid? Give details.

Have you ever fancied one of your mate's mothers and if so whose?
Who's the oldest woman you've ever entertained? What happened?
Where's the most unusual place you've had sex? Give details.
Have you ever slept with someone you shouldn't (best mate's girlfriend/married woman)? Did you get away with it?
What's the most embarrassing thing that's ever happened to you in front of a woman?
Have you ever been caught having sex with yourself?
What's the daftest tip someone's ever given you to increase your willy size?

Tip:

If you don't have an answer or don't want to answer then lie. You don't want to drink the revolting concoction, pass out and miss the juicy gossip.

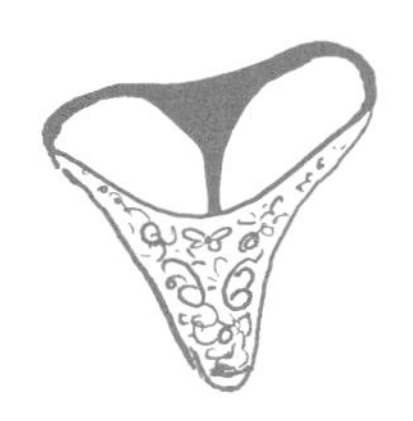

Pin the Nipples on the Boobs

Before you get busy:

Delve into your porn collection and find your favourite naked babe. Photocopy the picture and get it blown up to as big as possible.

Mould two small pieces of Blu-Tack or plasticine into nipples.

Get a blindfold.

How to play:

The aim of this game is to place *both* nipples in the correct place.

The guy who's closest wins a prize.

Possible prizes:

A personal performance from the stripper you've hired
A private lap dance if you go to a club
A copy of the famous Pammy and Tommy Lee video (by now it could be available on DVD)
A pair of fake boobs
A willy enlargement device
A book of chat-up lines

A willy warmer

A pair of women's frilly knickers (it's up to you whether they've been worn or not).

Tip:

If you're playing this at home, don't forget to take down the picture before your missus comes home. Ditto if you're living with your parents.

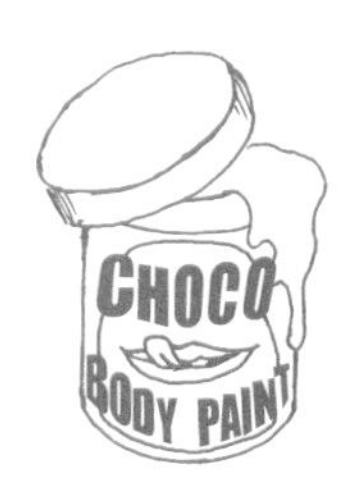

The Great Knicker Chase

How to play:

This is a contest to see who can collect the most pairs of knickers in one evening. Approach the wrong girl and it's smack-in-the-face time.

The rules:

You can't ask/steal from your sister or girlfriend. You can't steal knickers from washing lines. (Don't tell me you haven't thought about it.)

Bonus points for thongs.
Major bonus points if you speak to a girl who's not wearing any pants to begin with.
Major kudos if you sniff a girl's pants when she's standing in front of you.

Tip:

Women can hit even harder than guys when they're mad.

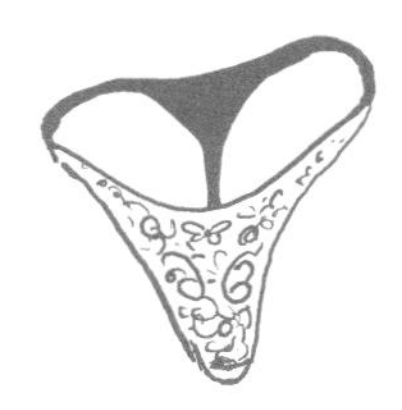

Pork Pie

You will need:

A pint of beer or lager
The contents of an overflowing ashtray
Some earwax

How to play:

You have to come out with a juicy statement about your sex life.

One player has to decide whether you're telling the truth by asking you questions.

Guess wrong and he pays the price by drinking the disgusting concoction. If he gets it right, it's you who has to drink.

Statements:

'I've slept with my girlfriend's mother/sister/best mate.'

'I once saw my parents getting it on.'

'I had sex with a nurse when I was visiting someone in hospital.'

'I once had three women at once.'

'I have regular spanking sessions with my girlfriend.'

'I tried on my girlfriend's underwear and she caught me.'

'I slept with that barmaid we all fancy.'

The Race

You will need:

A blow-up woman for each player

How to play:

It's a race to see who can inflate their lady the quickest.

Last guy gets tied to a lamppost, naked, at the mercy of peeing dogs in keeping with that longstanding stag night tradition. Even if it's not a stag night.

Make the task more difficult by:

Blowing whilst blindfolded.
Blowing whilst handcuffed.
Blowing whilst swigging from your beer glass.

'Can I Have Your Panties Please?'

You will need:

To get as drunk as you can (trust me, once you find out what you have to do you'll need some of the strong stuff)
A dummy or blow-up woman for each guy
A pair of handcuffs for everyone

How to play:

Every bloke has to be handcuffed to his woman.

Each guy has to have their doll dressed up by the end of the night using items of clothing donated by willing girls.

The rules:

Fail and you have to sleep with your plastic woman. But hey, it might be the only offer you get.

Tip:

Women are more likely to respond if you tell them what you're up to instead of just saying, 'Drop your knickers now.'

Chapter Eight
Rude Group Games

Get to know people better by inviting them round for drinks and nipples – I mean nibbles – and once lulled into a false sense of security by copious amounts of alcohol, spring some naughty games on them. They can run but they can't hide.

Ready? Let's go...

Rating – Games to get to know members of the opposite sex... intimately.

Consequences

You will need:

A group of friends
Paper and pens
A one-track mind

How to play:

Give everyone a piece of paper and a pen and sit in a circle. A series of questions is asked – Who, What, Where, When, Why and How. Once you have written down the answer to the first, fold the paper so the answer's concealed and then pass the paper on to the next person. Each time a question is answered the paper is folded and passed along to the next player.

Questions:

Who did you see? Choose two celebrities, or two people in the room.
What were they doing? This has to be something saucy or downright naughty.
Where did you see them? This works best if it's somewhere unusual or offbeat, like in an escalator.
When did you see it? The more unusual the answer the better, e.g. 'After I'd been stripping for them in a lap-dancing club.'

Why were they doing it? Keep it erotic: 'Because he couldn't keep his hands off her.'
How did it all turn out? Invent the consequences of their actions.
At the end, everyone reads their piece of paper with the combination of stories – with some hilarious results.

The rules:

Answers can be as naughty as you like. The naughtier the better.

This is an excuse to:

Indulge in some smutty talk.

Saucy Charades

How to play:

You may wonder, 'How the heck can anyone make charades saucy?' The answer is in the way you play.

Transform charades by making it a requirement that every puzzle has to be something sexy. It can be a film famous for its sex scenes (you have to act out the scene), the name of a sex toy, or something two (or more) people do between the sheets. The only limit is your imagination.

The rules:

If no one guesses right, you've got to pay the price.

Forfeits:

Come up with as many different uses for a condom as you can in one minute (using it as a bath cap, a party balloon, inflatable portable fish tank...)

Come up with as many different uses for a member of the opposite sex as you can

Describe a pair of breasts/a willy to everyone in the room as though they've never seen them/one before

Flash at everyone

Tip:

Deliberately make sure that no one gets your charade right, so you get to re-enact a famous sex scene with the hunk or babe you've got your eye on.

'Honey I Love You'

How to play:

Sit in a circle. One player is 'It' and has to sit on someone's knee and say, 'Honey I love you. If you love me smile,' and try to make that person laugh.

The person whose knee they are sitting on has to reply, 'Honey I love you but I just can't smile,' without smiling, laughing or showing any emotion. If they smile then that person becomes It.

The person who's It moves onto the next knee and so on until they succeed.

The rules:

No tickling!

This is an excuse for:

Listening to some delicious well-endowed stranger tell you he loves you without you having to sleep with him first.

Tip:

Rig it with your friends so that yours is the knee dream man sits on first.

Pass The Buck

You will need:

Some bananas
An assortment of sex toys
Some naughty nibbles

How to play:

You have to pass different objects around the room. Sounds easy, huh? Not when you're not allowed to use your hands.

The rules:

Suitable punishments should be dished out to people who drop the object, like having to take down someone's zip with their teeth.

This is an excuse for:

You to get all touchy-feely – all in the name of fun.

Tip:

If you want to make the game more difficult, pass a vibrator between players whilst it's switched on.

The Clothes Swapping Game

Before you strip:

Make sure you're wearing nice or no undies. Pair up. (Nab the person you fancy before your mate does.)

How to play:

Partners pair up and have to undress and change into the other's clothes in less than a minute.

Penalties should be agreed beforehand for go-slows.

This is an excuse for:

Members of the opposite sex to get to know each other better.

Finding out what kind of pants (if any) your eye-candy wears before you decide whether or not you want to sleep with them. Getting into their pants is what this game – and book – is all about after all.

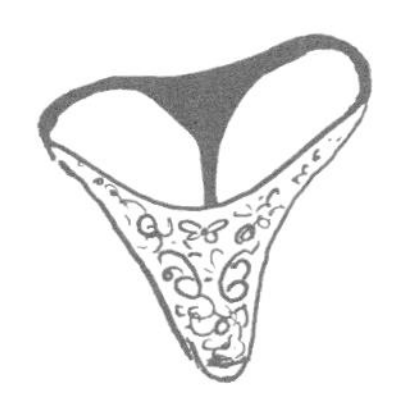